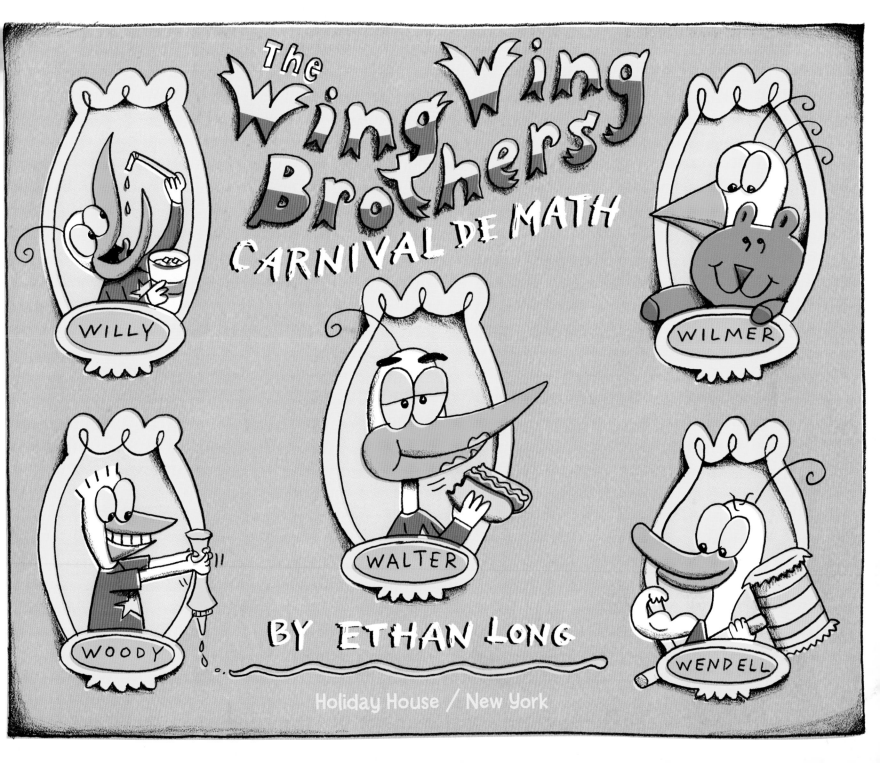

Willy tests his strength.

But he is a weakling. He scores a 10.

Now Woody wants to give it a whirl.

But he scores a 30. He is weak too.

Wilmer thinks he is way stronger.

He is stronger, but only a wee bit. He scores a 50.

Wendell wants a whack at it.

But his score of 90 is wimpy. Sorry, Wendell.

Walter walks over . . .

winds up . . .

and swings!

Walter scores 100! But not the way he wanted.

Wendell has 10 wieners.

Woody has 10 wieners.

Together they have 20 wieners. **10 + 10 = 20**

Wait! Wilmer has 20 wieners!

And Walter has 30!

There are 70 wieners now. Wow! **20 + 20 + 30 = 70**

What in the world? Willy has 30 wieners too!

Wendell, Wilmer, Willy, Walter, and Woody have 100 wieners.

70 + 30 = 100

But watch out!

It's a *wiener war!*

Wendell ate 10 wieners.
100 - 10 = 90

Woody ate 10 wieners.
90 - 10 = 80

Wilmer, Willy, and Walter have each eaten 10. But they want more.

$$80 - 10 - 10 - 10 = 50$$

Wilmer ate 0 more wieners.

$$50 - 0 = 50$$

Walter and Willy have both eaten 10 more wieners but are not winded.

$$50 - 10 - 10 = 30$$

Who'll be the winner?

They both ate 10 more wieners. But Walter feels woozy.

Can Willy eat the last 10 wieners?

YES! 10 - 10 = 0

Wendell, Wilmer, Willy, Walter, and Woody all need wider waistbands.

Walter, Woody, Wilmer, Wendell, and Willy wait at the Wedgie Wheel.

10 passengers get on.

0 + 10 = 10

10 more passengers get on. Now there are 20 passengers. **10 + 10 = 20**

But 10 more get on. **20 + 10 = 30**

And 10 more.

And another 10.

Now there are 50 passengers.

30 + 10 + 10 = 50

But wait!

10 more passengers get on!

50 + 10 = 60

Then 20 more . . .

60 + 20 = 80

And 20 more . . .

80 + 20 = 100

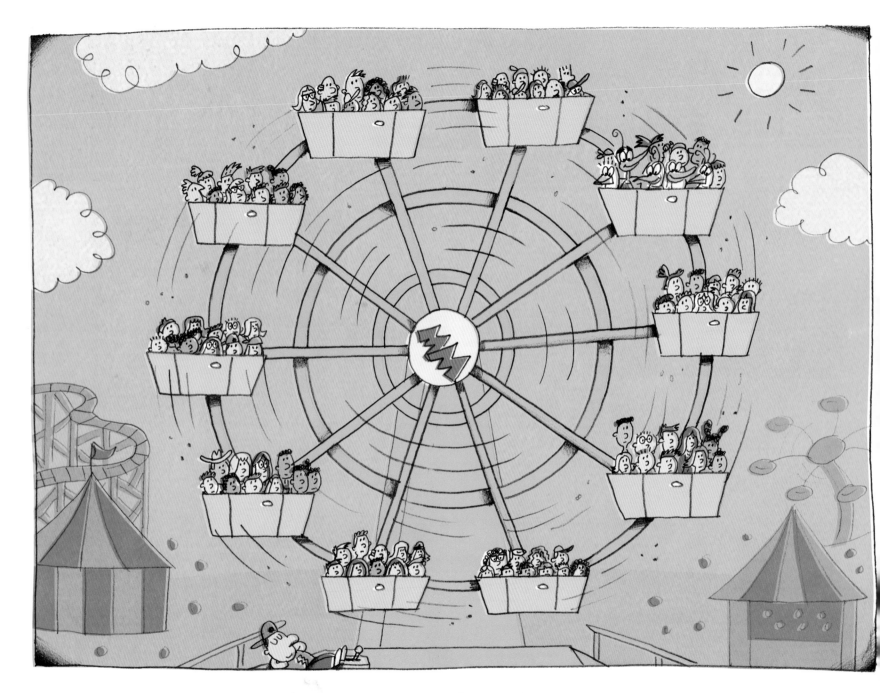

Wheee! The Wedgie Wheel is finally full! But not for long!

10 passengers want off... **100 – 10 = 90**

then 20 more... **90 – 20 = 70**

and 20 more... **70 – 20 = 50**

and 10 more . . .   and 10 more . . .   and 10 more . . .

and 10 more.   50 − 10 − 10 − 10 − 10 = 10

The Wing Wing brothers want their money's worth.

Be careful what you wish for!

What a wild weekend for the Wing Wing brothers! Wave good-bye!

The Common Core State Standards

This book meets the Common Core State Standards for kindergarten mathematics in Counting and Cardinality: K.CC.4 and K.CC4b. It also meets the Common Core State Standards for first-grade mathematics in Numbers and Operations in Base Ten: 1. NBT.4 and 1.NBT.6.

The publisher would like to thank Grace Wilkie, past president of the Association of Mathematics Teachers of New York State, for evaluating how this book meets the Common Core State Standards.

To Emel Partridge:
put some birds
on it.

Printed and Bound in October 2012 at Tien Wah Press,
Johor Bahru, Johor, Malaysia.
The text typeface is Billy.
The artwork was created with black Prismacolor pencils
on bristol board and colored digitally on a Mac.
www.holidayhouse.com
First Edition
1 3 5 7 9 10 8 6 4 2

Library of Congress Cataloging-in-Publication Data
Long, Ethan.
The Wing Wing brothers : carnival de math / Ethan Long. — 1st ed.
p. cm.
Audience: 4-8
ISBN 978-0-8234-2604-1 (hardcover)
1. Counting—Juvenile literature.
2. Cardinal numbers—Juvenile literature.
3. Ten (The number)—Juvenile literature. I. Title.
QA113.L66 2013
513.2'11—dc23
2012016562